Fall Leaves

Colorful and Crunchy

Martha E. H. Rustad

illustrated by Amanda Enright

M MILLBROOK PRESS · MINNEAPOLIS

For my sons, whose love of "I Spy"
inspired this book —M. E. H. R.

Millbrook Press
A division of Lerner Publishing Group, Inc.
241 First Avenue North
Minneapolis, MN 55401 U.S.A.

Website address: www.lernerbooks.com

Main body text set in Slappy Inline 18/28.
Typeface provided by T26.

Library of Congress Cataloging-in-Publication Data

Rustad, Martha E. H. (Martha Elizabeth Hillman), 1975–
    Fall leaves : colorful and crunchy / by Martha E. H. Rustad ;
illustrated by Amanda Enright.
        p.   cm. — (Cloverleaf books—Fall's here!)
    Includes index.
    ISBN 978–0–7613–5062–0 (lib. bdg. : alk. paper)
    1. Leaves—Juvenile literature. 2. Leaves—Color.
3. Autumn—Juvenile literature. I. Enright, Amanda, ill. II. Title.
QK649.R879 2011
581.4'8—dc22   2010053301

Manufactured in the United States of America
2 – BP – 8/1/12

TABLE OF CONTENTS

Chapter One

Looking at Leaves

Let's go on a **fall leaf hunt.**

Look! I spy one **red leaf.**
Do you know why leaves change color?
Let's look closely at leaves.

Look! I spy a web of **tiny lines.**
Those veins carry water through the leaf.

6

Leaves soak up sunlight.

They take in gas from the air through tiny holes.

Parts inside leaves make tree food with the gas, sunlight, and water. Veins carry the food back to the tree.

FOOD

Making food for the tree is called photosynthesis.

Chapter Two

Winter, Spring, Summer, Fall

Let's watch a tree as it **changes each season**. **Look!** I spy dry, scratchy branches.

In winter, many trees have no leaves. Trees look dead. They don't grow during cold, short winter days.

Evergreen trees keep their green, needle-shaped leaves all winter.

Look! I spy a **tiny bud** on a branch.

10

Spring days last longer.
Sunshine warms the buds.

Rain falls on the ground.
Water creeps up from the roots
to the trunk to the branches.

Look! I spy a little **green leaf.**

Bright summer sunlight and long days help leaves grow. Inside each leaf are lots of colors. But only green shows in summer.

Green bits inside leaves are called chlorophyll. They make tree food.

Look! I spy colorful fall leaves.
Cool fall days are shorter.
Leaves stop making food.
Their green color goes away.

Red, orange, yellow, and other colors show.
Bright leaves flutter in the breeze.

A tree's fall leaf color gives you a hint about what kind of tree it is. Maples have orange or red leaves. Birch and poplar have yellow leaves. Oak trees have mostly brown leaves.

Chapter Three

Falling Leaves

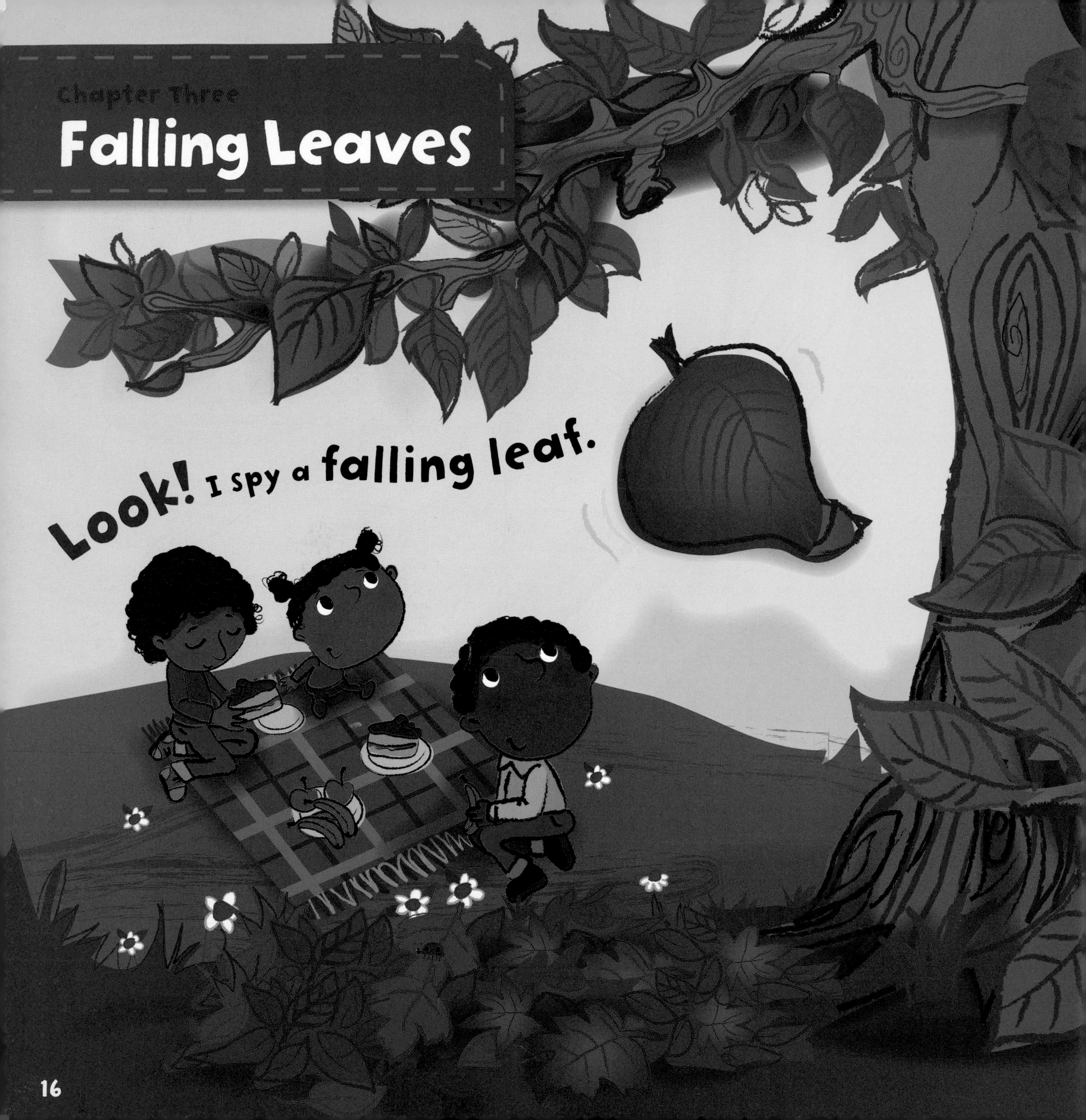

Look! I spy a **falling leaf.**

In fall, water stops going to the leaves. The part holding the leaf to the branch grows weak. The wind blows. The leaf falls.

The amount of sunlight and water a leaf gets depends on where the leaf hangs on a tree. So each leaf on a tree may change color and fall at a different time.

Dead leaves dry up and break apart.
Bits of the dead leaves sink into the soil.

These bits are nutrients. They are good for plants.

Roots gather the nutrients and bring them to growing plants.

Look! I spy a mark on the branch.

Tiny scars are left when leaves fall. Near each scar is a small bud that formed during summer.

During winter, bud scales cover the small buds. The scales protect buds from getting too cold and dry.

The buds wait all fall and winter.
In spring, new leaves grow.

The new leaves make more
food for the tree. They help
it grow and grow and grow.

Make a Leaf Print

Go on a leaf hunt when colors are brightest in the fall. Collect leaves for this easy art project! Then make sure an adult is around to help while you're making the leaf print.

Ingredients:
Colorful fall leaves (NOTE: This works best with leaves that are still fleshy and not dried out.)

Equipment:
watercolor paper (available at art stores)
paper towels
small hammer

Steps:

1) Choose a leaf with a bright or bold color.

2) Put the leaf on the watercolor paper. Cover it with a paper towel.

3) Gently tap the leaf all over with the hammer.

4) Peel away the paper towel and the leaf. Enjoy your leaf print!

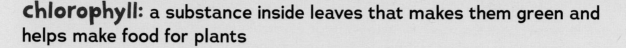

chlorophyll: a substance inside leaves that makes them green and helps make food for plants

gas: a substance, such as air, that spreads to fill any space that holds it. Leaves take in a gas called carbon dioxide from the air to make food for plants.

nutrient: something that helps living things, including plants, stay healthy

photosynthesis: the process by which leaves make food for plants from sunlight, water, and carbon dioxide

root: a part of a plant that spreads out below the ground. Roots pull up water from the soil.

scar: a mark on a branch left after a leaf falls

vein: a tiny tube inside a leaf. It carries water to the leaf and food to the tree.

BOOKS

Amoroso, Cynthia, and Robert B. Noyed. *Fall.* Mankato, MN: Child's World, 2010.
This short book introduces readers to the fall months with bright photos.

Anderson, Sheila. *Are You Ready for Fall?* Minneapolis: Lerner Publications Company,
2010. Get ready to put on a sweater, rake leaves, and harvest pumpkins! This book explores all
the things that happen in the fall.

Davis, Barbara J. *How Do Plants Get Food?* New York: Chelsea Clubhouse, 2010.
Color photos and illustrations show how plants use sunlight and water to make food through
photosynthesis.

WEBSITES

Photosynthesis for Kids
http://www.bbc.co.uk/gardening/gardening_with_children/didyouknow_photosynthesis.shtml
Discover fascinating facts about how plants grow, how they help the environment, and more.

Why Leaves Change Color in Fall
http://www.kidzone.ws/plants/autumn1.htm
Find out why fall weather turns leaves yellow, orange, red, or purple.

INDEX